# Introduction to the
# Metaphysic of Morals

# Introduction to the Metaphysic of Morals

by Immanuel Kant
translated by W. Hastie

Start Publishing PD is a registered trademark of Start Publishing PD LLC
Manufactured in the United States of America

Cover art: Shutterstock/Taisiya Kozorez

Cover design: Jennifer Do

10  9  8  7  6  5  4  3  2  1

ISBN 979-8-8809-0621-5

# Table of Contents

Division of the Metaphysic of Morals as a System of Duties Generally ....................................... 8

Division of the Metaphysic of Morals According to the Objective Relation of the Law of Duty. ............... 10

Division Possible According to the Subjective Relation of Those Who Bind under Obligations, and Those Who Are Bound under Obligations ............................... 12

Division of the Metaphysic of Morals as a System of Duties Generally ....................................... 14

The Relation of the Faculties of the Human Mind to the Moral Laws ........................................ 18

The Idea and Necessity of a Metaphysic of Morals ...... 25

The Division of a Metaphysic of Morals .............. 31

General Preliminary Conceptions Defined and Explained .. 36

# DIVISIONS:

## GENERAL DIVISIONS OF THE METAPHYSIC OF MORALS

# Division of the Metaphysic of Morals as a System of Duties Generally.

1. All duties are either duties of right, that is, juridical duties (officia juris), or duties of virtue, that is, ethical duties (officia virtutis s. ethica). Juridical duties are such as may be promulgated by external legislation; ethical duties are those for which such legislation is not possible. The reason why the latter cannot be properly made the subject of external legislation is because they relate to an end or final purpose, which is itself, at the same time, embraced in these duties, and which it is a duty for the individual to have as such. But no external legislation can cause any one to adopt a particular intention, or to propose to himself a certain purpose; for this depends upon an internal condition or act of the mind itself. However, external actions conducive to such a mental condition may be commanded, without its being implied that the individual will of necessity make them an end to himself.

But why, then, it may be asked, is the science of morals, or moral philosophy, commonly entitled— especially by Cicero— the science of duty and not also the science of right, since duties and rights refer to each other? The reason is this. We know our own freedom— from which all moral laws and consequently all rights as well as all duties arise— only through the moral imperative, which is an immediate injunction of duty; whereas the conception of right as a ground of putting others under obligation has afterwards to be developed out of it.

2. In the doctrine of duty, man may and ought to be represented in accordance with the nature of his faculty of freedom, which is entirely supra-sensible. He is, therefore, to be represented purely according to his humanity as a personality independent of physical determinations (homo noumenon), in distinction from the same person as a man modified with these determinations (homo phenomenon). Hence the conceptions of right and end when referred to duty, in view of this twofold quality, give the following division:

# Division of the Metaphysic of Morals According to the Objective Relation of the Law of Duty.

A. Juridical Duties to Oneself or Others

I. The Right of Humanity. in our own person (juridicial duties towards oneself) [Perfect Duty]

II. The Right of Mankind. in others (juridical duties towards others.) [Perfect Duty]

B. Ethical Duties to Oneself or Others

III. The End of Humanity. in our person (eithical duties toward oneself) [Imperfect Duty] IV. The End of Mankind. in others (ethical duties towards others.) [Imperfect Duty]

# Division of the Metaphysic of Morals According to Relations of Obligation.

As the subjects between whom a relation of right and duty is apprehended— whether it actually exists or not— admit of being conceived in various juridical relations to each other, another division may be proposed from this point of view, as follows:

# Division Possible According to the Subjective Relation of Those Who Bind under Obligations, and Those Who Are Bound under Obligations.

1. The juridical relation of man to beings who have neither right nor duty:

Vacat. There is no such relation, for such beings are irrational, and they neither put us under obligation, nor can we be put under obligation by them.

2. The juridical relation of man to beings who have both rights and duties:

Adest. There is such a relation, for it is the relation of men to men.

3. The juridical relation of man to beings who have only duties and no rights:

Vacat. There is no such relation, for such beings would be men without juridical personality, as slaves of bondsmen.

4 The juridical relation of man to a being who has only rights and no duties (God):

Vacat. There is no such relation in mere philosophy, because such a being is not an object of possible experience.

A real relation between right and duty is therefore found, in this scheme, only in No. 2. The reason why such is not likewise found in No. 4 is because it would constitute a transcendent duty, that is, one to which no corresponding subject can be given that is external and capable of imposing obligation. Consequently the relation from the theoretical point of view is here merely ideal; that is, it is a relation to an object of thought which we form for ourselves. But the conception of this object is not entirely empty. On the contrary, it is a fruitful conception in relation to ourselves and the maxims of our inner morality, and therefore in relation to practice generally. And it is in this bearing that all the duty involved and practicable for us in such a merely ideal relation lies.

# Division of the Metaphysic of Morals as a System of Duties Generally.

According to the constituent principles and the method of the system.

I. Principles
II. Duties of Right
III. Private Right.
IV. Public Right
V. Duties of Virtue, etc.

And so on, including all that refers not only to the materials, but also to the architectonic form of a scientific system of morals, when the metaphysical investigation of the elements has completely traced out the universal principles constituting the whole.

A. Method     B. Didactics     C. Ascetics

# General Introduction to the Metaphysic of Morals

# The Relation of the Faculties of the Human Mind to the Moral Laws.

The active faculty of the human mind, as the faculty of desire in its widest sense, is the power which man has, through his mental representations, of becoming the cause of objects corresponding to these representations. The capacity of a being to act in conformity with his own representations is what constitutes the life of such a being.

It is to be observed, first, that with desire or aversion there is always connected pleasure or pain, the susceptibility for which is called feeling. But the converse does not always hold; for there may be a pleasure connected, not with the desire of an object, but with a mere mental representation, it being indifferent whether an object corresponding to the representation exist or not. And second, the pleasure or pain connected with the object of desire does not always precede the activity of desire; nor can it be regarded in every case as the cause, but it may as well be the effect of that activity. The capacity of experiencing pleasure or pain on the occasion of a mental representation is called "feeling," because pleasure and pain contain only what is subjective in the relations of our mental activity. They do not involve any relation to an object that could possibly furnish a knowledge of it as such; they cannot even give us a knowledge of our own mental state. For even sensations,[The sensibility as the faculty of sense may be defined by reference to the subjective nature of our representations generally. It is the understanding that fir refers the subjective representations to an object; it alone thinks anything by means of these representations. Now, the subjective nature of our representations might be of such a kind that they could be related to objects so as to furnish knowledge of them, either in regard to their form or matter— in the former relation by pure perception, in the latter by sensation proper. In this case, the sense-faculty, as the capacity for receiving objective representations, would be properly called sense perception. But mere mental representation from its subjective nature cannot, in fact, become a constituent of objective knowledge, because it contains merely the relation of the representations to the subject, and includes nothing that can be used for attaining a knowledge of the object. In this case, then, this receptivity of the mind for subjective representations is called feeling. It includes the effect of the representations, whether sensible or intellectual, upon the subject; and it belongs to the sensibility, although the representation itself may belong to the understanding or the reason.] considered apart from the qualities which attach to them on account of the modifications of the subject— as, for instance, in reference to red, sweet, and such like— are referred as constituent elements of knowledge to objects, whereas pleasure or pain felt in connection with what is red or sweet express absolutely nothing that is in the object, but merely a relation to the subject. And for the reason just stated, pleasure and pain considered in themselves cannot be more precisely defined. All that can be further done with regard to them is merely to point out what consequences they may have in certain relations, in order to make the knowledge of them available practically.

The pleasure which is necessarily connected with the activity of desire, when the representation of the object desired affects the capacity of feeling, may be called practical pleasure. And this designation is applicable whether the pleasure is the cause or the effect of the desire. On the other hand, that pleasure which is not necessarily connected with the desire of an object, and which, therefore, is not a pleasure in the existence of the object, but is merely attached to a mental representation alone, may be called inactive complacency, or mere contemplative pleasure. The feeling of this latter kind of pleasure is what is called taste. Hence, in a system of practical philosophy, the contemplative pleasure of taste will not be discussed as an essential constituent conception, but need only be referred to incidentally or episodically. But as regards practical pleasure, it is otherwise. For the determination of the activity of the faculty of desire or appetency, which is necessarily preceded by this pleasure as its cause, is what properly constitutes desire in the strict sense of the term. Habitual desire, again, constitutes inclination; and the connection of pleasure with the activity of desire, in so far as this connection is judged by the understanding to be valid according to a general rule holding good at least for the individual, is what is called interest. Hence, in such a case, the practical pleasure is an interest of the inclination of the individual. On the other hand, if the pleasure can only follow a preceding determination of the faculty of desire, it is an intellectual pleasure, and the interest in the object must be called a rational interest; for were the interest sensuous, and not based only upon pure principles of reason, sensation would necessarily be conjoined with the pleasure, and would thus determine the activity of the desire. Where an entirely pure interest of reason must be assumed, it is not legitimate to introduce into it an interest of inclination surreptitiously. However, in order to conform so far with the common phraseology, we may allow the application of the term "inclination" even to that which can only be the object of an "intellectual" pleasure in the sense of a habitual desire arising from a pure interest of reason. But such inclination would have to be viewed, not as the cause, but as the effect of the rational interest; and we might call it the non-sensuous or rational inclination (propensio intellectualis). Further, concupiscence is to be distinguished from the activity of desire itself, as a stimulus or incitement to its determination. It is always a sensuous state of the mind, which does not itself attain to the definiteness of an act of the power of desire.

The activity of the faculty of desire may proceed in accordance with conceptions; and in so far as the principle thus determining it to action is found in the mind, and not in its object it constitutes a power acting or not acting according to liking. In so far as the activity is accompanied with the consciousness of the power of the action to produce the object, it forms an act of choice; if this consciousness is not conjoined with it, the activity is called a wish. The faculty of desire, in so far as its inner principle of determination as the ground of its liking or predilection lies in the reason of the subject, constitutes the will. The will is therefore the faculty of active desire or appetency, viewed not so much in relation to the action— which is the relation of the act of choice— as rather in relation to the principle that determines the power of choice to the action. It has, in itself, properly no special principle of determination, but in so far as it may determine the voluntary act of choice, it is the practical reason itself.

Under the will, taken generally, may be included the volitional act of choice, and also the mere act of wish, in so far as reason may determine the faculty of desire in its activity. The act of choice that can be determined by pure reason constitutes the act of free-will. That act which is determinable only by inclination as a sensuous impulse or stimulus would be irrational brute choice (arbitrium brutum). The human act of choice, however, as human, is in fact affected by such impulses or stimuli, but is not determined by them; and it is, therefore, not pure in itself when taken apart from the acquired habit of determination by reason. But it may be determined to action by the pure will. The freedom of the act of volitional choice is its independence of being determined by sensuous impulses or stimuli. This forms the negative conception of the free-will. The positive conception of freedom is given by the fact that the will is the capability of pure reason to be practical of itself. But this is not possible otherwise than by the maxim of every action being subjected to the condition of being practicable as a universal law. Applied as pure reason to the act of choice, and considered apart from its objects, it may be regarded as the faculty of principles; and, in this connection, it is the source of practical principles. Hence it is to be viewed as a law-giving faculty. But as the material upon which to construct a law is not furnished to it, it can only make the form of the form of the maxim of the act of will, in so far as it is available as a universal law, the supreme law and determining principle of the will. And as the maxims, or rules of human action derived from subjective causes, do not of themselves necessarily agree with those that are objective and universal, reason can only prescribe this supreme law as an absolute imperative of prohibition or command.

The laws of freedom, as distinguished from the laws of nature, are moral laws. So far as they refer only to external actions and their lawfulness, they are called juridical; but if they also require that, as laws, they shall themselves be the determining principles of our actions, they are ethical. The agreement of an action with juridical laws is its legality; the agreement of an action with ethical laws is its morality. The freedom to which the former laws refer, can only be freedom in external practice; but the freedom to which the latter laws refer is freedom in the internal as well as the external exercise of the activity of the will in so far as it is determined by laws of reason. So, in theoretical philosophy, it is said that only the objects of the external senses are in space, but all the objects both of internal and external sense are in time; because the representations of both, as being representations, so far belong all to the internal sense. In like manner, whether freedom is viewed in reference to the external or the internal action of the will, its laws, as pure practical laws of reason for the free activity of the will generally, must at the same time be inner principles for its determination, although they may not always be considered in this relation.

# The Idea and Necessity of a Metaphysic of Morals.

It has been shown in The Metaphysical Principles of the Science of Nature that there must be principles a priori for the natural science that has to deal with the objects of the external senses. And it was further shown that it is possible, and even necessary, to formulate a system of these principles under the name of a "metaphysical science of nature," as a preliminary to experimental physics regarded as natural science applied to particular objects of experience. But this latter science, if care be taken to keep its generalizations free from error, may accept many propositions as universal on the evidence of experience, although if the term "universal" be taken in its strict sense, these would necessarily have to be deduced by the metaphysical science from principles a priori. Thus Newton accepted the principle of the equality of action and reaction as established by experience, and yet he extended it as a universal law over the whole of material nature. The chemists go even farther, grounding their most general laws regarding the combination and decomposition of the materials of bodies wholly upon experience; and yet they trust so completely to the universality and necessity of those laws that they have no anxiety as to any error being found in propositions founded upon experiments conducted in accordance with them.

But it is otherwise with moral laws. These, in

contradistinction to natural laws, are only valid as laws, in so far as they can be rationally established a priori and comprehended as necessary. In fact, conceptions and judgements regarding ourselves and our conduct have no moral significance, if they contain only what may be learned from experience; and when any one is, so to speak, misled into making a moral principle out of anything derived from this latter source, he is already in danger of falling into the coarsest and most fatal errors.

If the philosophy of morals were nothing more than a theory of happiness (eudaemonism), it would be absurd to search after principles a priori as a foundation for it. For however plausible it may sound to say that reason, even prior to experience, can comprehend by what means we may attain to a lasting enjoyment of the real pleasures of life, yet all that is taught on this subject a priori is either tautological, or is assumed wholly without foundation. It is only experience that can show what will bring us enjoyment. The natural impulses directed towards nourishment, the sexual instinct, or the tendency to rest and motion, as well as the higher desires of honour, the acquisition of knowledge, and such like, as developed with our natural capacities, are alone capable of showing in what those enjoyments are to be found. And, further, the knowledge thus acquired is available for each individual merely in his own way; and it is only thus he can learn the means by which be has to seek those enjoyments. All specious rationalizing a priori, in this connection, is nothing at bottom but carrying facts of experience up to generalizations by induction (secundum principia generalia non universalia); and the generality thus attained is still so limited that numberless exceptions must be allowed to every individual in order that he may adapt the choice of his mode of life to his own Particular inclinations and his capacity for pleasure. And, after all, the individual has really to acquire his prudence at the cost of his own suffering or that of his neighbors the form

But it is quite otherwise with the principles of morality. They lay down commands for every one without regard to his particular inclinations, and merely because and so far as he is free, and has a practical reason. Instruction in the laws of morality is not drawn from observation of oneself or of our animal nature, nor from perception of the course of the world in regard to what happens, or how men act.* But reason commands how we ought to act, even although no example of such action were to be found; nor does reason give any regard to the advantage which may accrue to us by so acting, and which experience could alone actually show. For, although reason allows us to seek what is for our advantage in every possible way, and although, founding upon the evidence of experience, it may further promise that greater advantages will probably follow on the average from the observance of her commands than from their transgression, especially if prudence guides the conduct, yet the authority of her precepts as commands does not rest on such considerations. They are used by reason only as counsels, and by way of a counterpoise against seductions to an opposite course, when adjusting beforehand the equilibrium of a partial balance in the sphere of practical judgement, in order thereby to secure the decision of this judgement, according to the due weight of the a priori principles of a pure practical reason.

*This holds notwithstanding the fact that the term morals," in Latin mores, and in German sitten, signifies originally only manners or mode of life.

Metaphysics designates any system of knowledge a priori that consists of pure conceptions. Accordingly, a practical philosophy not having nature, but the freedom of the will for its object, will presuppose and require a metaphysic of morals. It is even a duty to have such a metaphysic; and every man does, indeed, possess it in himself, although commonly but in an obscure way. For how could any one believe that he has a source of universal law in himself, without principles a priori? And just as in a metaphysics of nature there must be principles regulating the application of the universal supreme principles of nature to objects of experience, so there cannot but be such principles in the metaphysic of morals; and we will often have to deal objectively with the particular nature of man as known only by experience, in order to show in it the consequences of these universal moral principles. But this mode of dealing with these principles in their particular applications will in no way detract from their rational purity, or throw doubt on their a priori origin. In other words, this amounts to saying that a metaphysic of morals cannot be founded on anthropology as the empirical science of man, but may be applied to it.

The counterpart of a metaphysic of morals, and the other member of the division of practical philosophy, would be a moral anthropology, as the empirical science of the moral nature of man. This science would contain only the subjective conditions that hinder or favor the realization in practice of the universal moral laws in human nature, with the means of propagating, spreading, and strengthening the moral principles— as by the education of the young and the instruction of the people— and all other such doctrines and precepts founded upon experience and indispensable in themselves, although they must neither precede the metaphysical investigation of the principles of reason, nor be mixed up with it. For, by doing so, there would be a great danger of laying down false, or at least very flexible moral laws, which would hold forth as unattainable what is not attached only because the law has not been comprehended and presented in its purity, in which also its strength consists. Or, otherwise, spurious and mixed motives might be adopted instead of what is dutiful and good in itself; and these would furnish no certain moral principles either for the guidance of the judgement or for the discipline of the heart in the practice of duty. It is only by pure reason, therefore, that duty can and must be prescribed.

The higher division of philosophy, under which the division just mentioned stands, is into theoretical philosophy and practical philosophy. Practical philosophy is just moral philosophy in its widest sense, as has been explained elsewhere.[In the Critique of Judgement (1790).] All that is practicable and possible, according to natural laws, is the special subject of the activity of art, and its precepts and rules entirely depend on the theory of nature. It is only what is practicable according to laws of freedom that can have principles independent of theory, for there is no theory in relation to what passes beyond the determinations of nature. Philosophy therefore cannot embrace under its practical division a technical theory, but only a morally practical doctrine. But if the dexterity of the will in acting according to laws of freedom, in contradistinction to nature, were to be also called an art, it would necessarily indicate an art which would make a system of freedom possible like the system of nature. This would truly be a Divine art, if we were in a position by means of it to realize completely what reason prescribes to us, and to put the idea into practice.

# The Division of a Metaphysic of Morals.

All legislation, whether relating to internal or external action, and whether prescribed a priori by mere reason or laid down by the will of another, involves two elements: First, a law which represents the action that ought to happen as necessary objectively, thus making the action a duty; second, a motive which connects the principle determining the will to this action with the mental representation of the law subjectively, so that the law makes duty the motive of the action. By the first element, the action is represented as a duty, in accordance with the mere theoretical knowledge of the possibility of determining the activity of the will by practical rules. By the second element, the obligation so to act is connected in the subject with a determining principle of the will as such. All legislation, therefore, may be differentiated by reference to its motive-principle.[This ground of division will apply, although the action which it makes a duty may coincide with another action that may be otherwise looked at from another point of view. For instance, actions may in all cases be classified as external.] The legislation which makes an action a duty, and this duty at the same time a motive, is ethical. That legislation which does not include the motive-principle in the law, and consequently admits another motive than the idea of duty itself, is juridical. In respect of the latter, it is evident that the motives distinct from the idea of duty, to which it may refer, must be drawn from the subjective (pathological) influences of inclination and of aversion, determining the voluntary activity, and especially from the latter; because it is a legislation which has to be compulsory, and not merely a mode of attracting or persuading. The agreement or non-agreement of an action with the law, without reference to its motive, is its legality; and that character of the action in which the idea of duty arising from the law at the same time forms the motive of the action, is its morality.

Duties specially in accord with a juridical legislation can only be external duties. For this mode of legislation does not require that the idea of the duty, which is internal, shall be of itself the determining principle of the act of will; and as it requires a motive suitable to the nature of its laws, it can only connect what is external with the law. Ethical legislation, on the other hand, makes internal actions also duties, but not to the exclusion of the external, for it embraces everything which is of the nature of duty. And just because just because ethical legislation includes within its law the internal motive of the action as contained in the idea of duty, it involves a characteristic which cannot at all enter into the legislation that is external. Hence, ethical legislation cannot as such be external, not even when proceeding from a Divine will, although it may receive duties which rest on an external legislation as duties, into the position of motives, within its own legislation.

From what has been said, it is evident that all duties, merely because they are duties, belong to ethics; and yet the legislation upon which they are founded is not on that account in all cases contained in ethics. On the contrary, the law of many of them lies outside of ethics. Thus ethics commands that I must fulfil a promise entered into by contract, although the other party might not be able to compel me to do so. It adopts the law (pacta sunt servanda) and the duty corresponding to it, from jurisprudence or the science of right, by which they are established. It is not in ethics, therefore, but in jurisprudence, that the principle of the legislation lies, that "promises made and accepted must be kept." Accordingly, ethics specially teaches that if the motive-principle of external compulsion which juridical legislation connects with a duty is even let go, the idea of duty alone is sufficient of itself as a motive. For were it not so, and were the legislation itself not juridical, and consequently the duty arising from it not specially a duty of right as distinguished from a duty of virtue, then fidelity in the performance of acts, to which the individual may be bound by the terms of a contract, would have to be classified with acts of benevolence and the obligation that underlies them, which cannot be correct. To keep one's promise is not properly a duty of virtue, but a duty of right, and the performance of it can be enforced by external compulsion. But to keep one's promise, even when no compulsion can be applied to enforce it, is, at the same time, a virtuous action, and a proof of virtue. jurisprudence as the science of right, and ethics as the science of virtue, are therefore distinguished not so much by their different duties, as rather by the difference Of the legislation which connects the one or the other kind of motive with their laws.

Ethical legislation is that which cannot be external, although the duties it prescribes may be external as well as internal. Juridical legislation is that which may also be external. Thus it is an external duty to keep a promise entered into by contract; but the injunction to do this merely because it is a duty, without regard to any other motive, belongs exclusively to the internal legislation. It does not belong thus to the ethical sphere as being a particular kind of duty or a particular mode of action to which we are bound— for it is an external duty in ethics as well as in jurisprudence— but it is because the legislation in the case referred to is internal, and cannot have an external lawgiver, that the obligation is reckoned as belonging to ethics. For the same reason, the duties of benevolence, although they are external duties as obligations to external actions, are, in like manner, reckoned as belonging to ethics, because they can only be enjoined by legislation that is internal. Ethics has no doubt its own peculiar duties— such as those towards oneself— but it bas also duties in common with jurisprudence, only not under the same mode of obligation. In short, the peculiarity of ethical legislation is to enjoin the performance of certain actions merely because they are duties, and to make the principle of duty itself— whatever be its source or occasion— the sole sufficing motive of the activity of the will. Thus, then, there are many ethical duties that are directly such; and the inner legislation also makes the others— all and each of them— indirectly ethical.

The deduction of the division of a system is the proof of its completeness as well as of its continuity, so that there may be a logical transition from the general conception divided to the members of the division, and through the whole series of the subdivisions without any break or leap in the arrangement (divisio per saltum). Such a division is one of the most difficult conditions for the architect of a system to fulfil. There is even some doubt as to what is the highest conception that is primarily divided into right and wrong (aut fas aut nefas). It is assuredly the conception of the activity of the free-will in general. In like manner, the expounders of ontology start from something and nothing, without perceiving that these are already members of a division for which the highest divided conception is awanting, and which can be no other than that of thing in general.

# General Preliminary Conceptions Defined and Explained.

(Philosophia practica universalis).

The conception of freedom is a conception of pure reason. It is therefore transcendent in so far as regards theoretical philosophy; for it is a conception for which no corresponding instance or example can be found or supplied in any possible experience. Accordingly freedom is not presented as an object of any theoretical knowledge that is possible for us. It is in no respect a constitutive, but only a regulative conception; and it can be accepted by the speculative reason as at most a merely negative principle. In the practical sphere of reason, however, the reality of freedom may be demonstrated by certain practical principles which, as laws, prove a causality of the pure reason in the process of determining the activity of the will that is independent of all empirical and sensible conditions. And thus there is established the fact of a pure will existing in us as the source of all moral conceptions and laws.

On this positive conception of freedom in the practical relation certain unconditional practical laws are founded, and they specially constitute moral laws. In relation to us as human beings, with an activity of will modified by sensible influences so as not to be conformable to the pure will, but as often contrary to it, these laws appear as imperatives commanding or prohibiting certain actions; and as such they are categorical or unconditional imperatives. Their categorical and unconditional character distinguishes them from the technical imperatives which express the prescriptions of art, and which always command only conditionally. According to these categorical imperatives, certain actions are allowed or disallowed as being morally possible or impossible; and certain of them or their opposites are morally necessary and obligatory. Hence, in reference to such actions, there arises the conception of a duty whose observance or transgression is accompanied with a pleasure or pain of a peculiar kind, known as moral feeling. We do not, however, take the moral feelings or sentiments into account in considering the practical laws of reason. For they do not form the foundation or principle of practical laws of reason, but only the subjective effects that arise in the mind on the occasion of our voluntary activity being determined by these laws. And while they neither add to nor take from the objective validity or influence of the moral laws in the judgement of reason, such sentiments may vary according to the differences of the individuals who experience them.

The following conceptions are common to jurisprudence and ethics as the two main divisions of the metaphysic of morals.

Obligation is the necessity of a free action when viewed in relation to a categorical imperative of reason. An imperative is a practical rule by which an action, otherwise contingent in itself, is made necessary. It is distinguished from a practical law in that such a law, while likewise representing the action as necessary, does not consider whether it is internally necessary as involved in the nature of the agent— say as a holy being— or is contingent to him, as in the case of man as we find him; for where the first condition holds good, there is in fact no imperative. Hence an imperative is a rule which not only represents but makes a subjectively contingent action necessary; and it, accordingly, represents the subject as being (morally) necessitated to act in accordance with this rule. A categorical or unconditional imperative is one which does not represent the action in any way immediately through the conception of an end that is to be attained by it; but it presents the action to the mind as objectively necessary by the mere representation of its form as an action, and thus makes it necessary. Such imperatives cannot be put forward by any other practical science than that which prescribes obligations, and it is only the science of morals that does this. All other imperatives are technical, and they are altogether conditional. The ground of the possibility of categorical imperatives lies in the fact that they refer to no determination of the activity of the will by which a purpose might be assigned to it, but solely to its freedom.

Every action is allowed (licitum) which is not contrary to obligation; and this freedom not being limited by an opposing imperative, constitutes a moral right as a warrant or title of action (facultas moralis). From this it is at once evident what actions are disallowed or illicit (illicita).

Duty is the designation of any action to which anyone is bound by an obligation. It is therefore the subject-matter of all obligation. Duty as regards the action concerned may be one and the same, and yet we may be bound to it in various ways.

The categorical imperative, as expressing an obligation in respect to certain actions, is a morally practical law. But because obligation involves not merely practical necessity expressed in a law as such, but also actual necessitation, the categorical imperative is a law either of command or prohibition, according as the doing or not doing of an action is represented as a duty. An action which is neither commanded nor forbidden is merely allowed, because there is no law restricting freedom, nor any duty in respect of it. Such an action is said to be morally indifferent (indifferens, adiaphoron, res merae facultatis). It may be asked whether there are such morally indifferent actions; and if there are, whether in addition to the preceptive and prohibitive law (lex praeceptiva et prohibitiva, lex mandati et vetiti), there is also required a permissive law (lex permissiva), in order that one may be free in such relations to act, or to forbear from acting, at his pleasure? If it were so, the moral right in question would not, in all cases, refer to actions that are indifferent in themselves (adiaphora); for no special law would be required to establish such a right, considered according to moral laws.

An action is called an act— or moral deed— in so far as it is subject to laws of obligation, and consequently in so far as the subject of it is regarded with reference to the freedom of his choice in the exercise of his will. The agent— as the actor or doer of the deed— is regarded as, through the act, the author of its effect; and this effect, along with the action itself, may be imputed to him, if be previously knew the law in virtue of which an obligation rested upon him.

A person is a subject who is capable of having his actions imputed to him. Moral personality is, therefore, nothing but the freedom of a rational being under moral laws; and it is to be distinguished from psychological freedom as the mere faculty by which we become conscious of ourselves in different states of the identity of our existence. Hence it follows that a person is properly subject to no other laws than those he lays down for himself, either alone or in conjunction with others.

A thing is what is incapable of being the subject of imputation. Every object of the free activity of the will, which is itself void of freedom, is therefore called a thing (res corporealis).

Right or wrong applies, as a general quality, to an act (rectum aut minus rectum), in so far as it is in accordance with duty or contrary to duty (factum licitum aut illicitum), no matter what may be the subject or origin of the duty itself. An act that is contrary to duty is called a transgression (reatus).

An unintentional transgression of a duty, which is, nevertheless, imputable to a person, is called a mere fault (culpa). An intentional transgression— that is, an act accompanied with the consciousness that it is a transgression— constitutes a crime (dolus).

Whatever is juridically in accordance with external laws is said to be just (jus, instum); and whatever is not juridically in accordance with external laws is unjust (unjustum).

A collision of duties or obligations (collisio officiorum s. obligationum) would be the result of such a relation between them that the one would annul the other, in whole or in part. Duty and obligation, however, are conceptions which express the objective practical necessity of certain actions, and two opposite rules cannot be objective and necessary at the same time; for if it is a duty to act according to one of them, it is not only no duty to act according to an opposite rule, but to do so would even be contrary to duty. Hence a collision of duties and obligations is entirely inconceivable (obligationes non colliduntur). There may, however, be two grounds of obligation (rationes obligandi), connected with an individual under a rule prescribed for himself, and yet neither the one nor the other may be sufficient to constitute an actual obligation (rationes obligandi non obligantes); and in that case the one of them is not a duty. If two such grounds of obligation are actually in collision with each other, practical philosophy does not say that the stronger obligation is to keep the upper hand (fortior obligatio vincit), but that the stronger ground of obligation is to maintain its place (fortior obligandi ratio vincit).

Obligatory Laws for which an external legislation is possible are called generally external laws. Those external laws, the obligatoriness of which can be recognised by reason a priori even without an external legislation, are called natural laws. Those laws, again, which are not obligatory without actual external legislation, are called positive laws. An external legislation, containing pure natural laws, is therefore conceivable; but in that case a previous natural law must be presupposed to establish the authority of the lawgiver by the right to subject others to obligation through his own act of will.

The principle which makes a certain action a duty is a practical law. The rule of the agent or actor, which he forms as a principle for himself on subjective grounds, is called his maxim. Hence, even when the law is one and invariable, the maxims of the agent may yet be very different.

The categorical imperative only expresses

generally what constitutes obligation. It may be rendered by the following formula: "Act according to a maxim which can be adopted at the same time as a universal law." Actions must therefore be considered, in the first place, according to their subjective principle; but whether this principle is also valid objectively can only be known by the criterion of the categorical imperative. For reason brings the principle or maxim of any action to the test, by calling upon the agent to think of himself in connection with it as at the same time laying down a universal law, and to consider whether his action is so qualified as to be fit for entering into such a universal legislation.

The simplicity of this law, in comparison with the great and manifold consequences which may be drawn from it, as well as its commanding authority and supremacy without the accompaniment of any visible motive or sanction, must certainly at first appear very surprising. And we may well wonder at the power of our reason to determine the activity of the will by the mere idea of the qualification of a maxim for the universality of a practical law, especially when we are taught thereby that this practical moral law first reveals a property of the will which the speculative reason would never have come upon either by principles a priori, or from any experience whatever; and even if it had ascertained the fact, it could never have theoretically established its possibility. This practical law, however, not only discovers the fact of that property of the will, which is freedom, but irrefutably establishes it. Hence it will be less surprising to find that the moral laws are undemonstrable, and yet apodeictic, like the mathematical postulates; and that they, at the same time, open up before us a whole field of practical knowledge, from which reason, on its theoretical side, must find itself entirely excluded with its speculative idea of freedom and all such ideas of the supersensible generally.

The conformity of an action to the law of duty constitutes its legality; the conformity of the maxim of the action with the law constitutes its morality. A maxim is thus a subjective principle of action, which the individual makes a rule for himself as to how in fact he will act. On the other hand, the principle of duty is what reason absolutely, and therefore objectively and universally, lays down in the form of a command to the individual, as to how he ought to act.

The supreme principle of the science of morals accordingly is this: "Act according to a maxim which can likewise be valid as a universal law." Every maxim which is not qualified according to this condition is contrary to Morality.

Laws arise from the will, viewed generally as practical reason; maxims spring from the activity of the will in the process of choice. The latter in man is what constitutes free-will. The will which refers to nothing else than mere law can neither be called free nor not free, because it does not relate to actions immediately, but to the giving of a law for the maxim of actions; it is therefore the practical reason itself. Hence as a faculty, it is absolutely necessary in itself, and is not subject to any external necessitation. It is, therefore, only the act of choice in the voluntary process that can be called free.

The freedom of the act of will, however, is not to be defined as a liberty of indifference (libertas indifferentae), that, is, as a capacity of choosing to act for or against the law. The voluntary process, indeed, viewed as a phenomenal appearance, gives many examples of this choosing in experience; and some have accordingly so defined the free-will. For freedom, as it is first made knowable by the moral law, is known only as a negative property in us, as constituted by the fact of not being necessitated to act by sensible principles of determination. Regarded as a noumenal reality, however, in reference to man as a pure rational intelligence, the act of the will cannot be at all theoretically exhibited; nor can it therefore be explained how this power can act necessitatingly in relation to the sensible activity in the process of choice, or consequently in what the positive quality of freedom consists. Only thus much we can see into and comprehend, that although man, as a being belonging to the world of sense, exhibits— as experience shows— a capacity of choosing not only conformably to the law but also contrary to it, his freedom as a rational being belonging to the world of intelligence cannot be defined by reference merely to sensible appearances. For sensible phenomena cannot make a super-sensible object— such as free-will is— intelligible; nor can freedom ever be placed in the mere fact that the rational subject can make a choice in conflict with his own law-giving reason, although experience may prove that it happens often enough, notwithstanding our inability to conceive how it is possible. For it is one thing to admit a proposition as based on experience, and another thing to make it the defining principle and the universal differentiating mark of the act of free-will, in its distinction from the arbitrium brutum s. servum;

because the empirical proposition does not assert that any particular characteristic necessarily belongs to the conception in question, but this is requisite in the process of definition. Freedom in relation to the internal legislation of reason can alone be properly called a power; the possibility of diverging from the law thus given is an incapacity or want of power. How then can the former be defined by the latter? It could only be by a definition which would add to the practical conception of the free-will, its exercise as shown by experience; but this would be a hybrid definition which would exhibit the conception in a false light.

A morally practical law is a proposition which contains a categorical imperative or command. He who commands by a law (imperans) is the lawgiver or legislator. He is the author of the obligation that accompanies the law, but he is not always the author of the law itself. In the latter case, the law would be positive, contingent, and arbitrary. The law which is imposed upon us a priori and unconditionally by our own reason may also be expressed as proceeding from the will of a supreme lawgiver or the Divine will. Such a will as supreme can consequently have only rights and not duties; and it only indicates the idea of a moral being whose will is law for all, without conceiving of him as the author of that will.

Imputation, in the moral sense, is the judgement by which anyone is declared to be the author or free cause of an action which is then regarded as his moral fact or deed, and is subjected to law. When the judgement likewise lays down the juridical consequences of the deed, it is judicial or valid (imputatio judiciaria s. valida); otherwise it would be only adjudicative or declaratory (imputatio dijudicatoria). That person— individual or collective— who is invested with the right to impute actions judicially, is called a judge or a court (judex s. forum).

When any one does, in conformity with duty, more than he can be compelled to do by the law, it is said to be meritorious (meritum). What is done only in exact conformity with the law, is what is due (debitum). And when less is done than can be demanded to be done by the law, the result is moral demerit (demeritum) or culpability.

The juridical effect or consequence of a culpable act of demerit is punishment (paena); that of a meritorious act is reward (praemium), assuming that this reward was promised in the law and that it formed the motive of the action. The coincidence or exact conformity of conduct to what is due has no juridical effect. Benevolent remuneration (remuneratio s. repensio benefica) has no place in juridical relations.

The good or bad consequences arising from the performance of an obligated action— as also the consequences arising from failing to perform a meritorious action— cannot be imputed to the agent (modus imputation is tollens). The good consequences of a meritorious action— as also the bad consequences of a wrongful action— may be imputed to the agent (modus imputation is poneus).

The degree of the imputability of actions is to be reckoned according to the magnitude of the hindrances or obstacles which it has been necessary for them to overcome. The greater the natural hindrances in the sphere of sense, and the less the moral hindrance of duty, so much the more is a good deed imputed as meritorious. This may be seen by considering such examples as rescuing a man who is an entire stranger from great distress, and at very considerable sacrifice. Conversely, the less the natural hindrance, and the greater the hindrance on the ground of duty, so much the more is a transgression imputable as culpable. Hence the state of mind of the agent or doer of a deed makes a difference in imputing its consequences, according as he did it in passion or performed it with coolness and deliberation.